LIFE-SIZED

SPAM Press
Glasgow 2025

ISBN: 978-1-915049-32-2
Cover art by Elisa de la Serna Gallego

Do we all experience this? Not just can we, do we?

Norman Rosenthal

BREAD EGG EGGSHELL

WHAT YOU DO FOR LIVING

He's what's happening
in this porous and
perverted light
if you prefer liquid factors to lightbulbs
the immediate hard-on of
Jeff's work
is something to look forward to

I'm a dirty old man succumbing to the temptation
of transness
watch stranger's feet
touch on the subway
Maria said critiquing something means
paying attention means loving I love your
self-mythologizing bent
flood of subject mistaking shine
for depth and stupid bracelets

Encounters with him are
like a soft damaged toy

my values include
fashioning small
holes in the blimp

The best thing about art is
when lesbians use it for kindle
Hulk/Elvis kind of night but the day was all
sitting in medical rooms with people who
are incredibly important and no one has
ever heard of yes I would like to keep
myself in a permanent state of want

It's in the split-rocker's nature to look
both ways
the rocking horse's eye looks to the right
and the dinosaur's eye looks forward
how's that for a two-dimensional sculpture
the interface where an overlap occurs
like watching the grass rise after
he's stepped on it

An aesthetic response of little resolve
where to look what to do
let's assume at least for
now that
the big picture isn't a square
or a knife the lockscreen
on your phone
but something
more like oil pooling
out of yellow bulbs
a slithery orange
that dies with the sun

SPLIT-ROCKER SNOWGLOBE

Drape a woman in cereal lavish her with potatoes

suppose the dense tableau of toy figurines were

to actually mean something

I flatten all my

exchanges like water jetting from a spring

at the end of the day it got loose and flew

down the street into our garden nightfall merges

Jeff pulling out with

last meal's memory

Belly button piercings

at the gallery opening

watch you openly flirt with

apple juice coating your top lip

I know you love me but

what about cobwebs on the Phyllida

Barlow

toy-camera operations passing days

paper jams half of

G-Ma's face

screaming back at you

I meet Jeff for

coffee

I tell him you jammed my heart he

says

like all the boys aren't cooking the books

there's a thud he leaves behind a model

half-dinosaur half-horse

observing the distance between what I want

and what tends to happen till

it's a toothpaste-sized dollop

I imagine in primitive times people

looked at their kill and noticed gases

expanding in their stomachs and

realized they could work with

this type of membrane

pumped air and plastic surface ripped

pants bulging muscles shivers of

trans frisson

It's a toy's difference between testosterone

and experimental gamma rays when both

turn you into a gang of green monsters

The cheap shit you buy

for your little cousin to

instantly pierce with

an overgrown toenail

like a home-grown lancet

Jeff somewhere in the garden

noting on the to-go cup that

it's been a very quiet morning

the kangaroo remains orange

the sheep yellow

you can beam light

references into the poem

or you can just swallow the

                    child's world whole

watch him nearly flinch but remain

still unscrupulously epic

You want a story something with form

he makes steel objects look like balloons

it's this masturbation technique where

you take a pin and let the air hiss out

meanwhile I'm stuck up in the

World of Allegory

gesticulating on the

other side of the stream

Hello how are you rosy-cheeked children

burning Thomas Lawrence paintings

oily hands touch the soles

of my feet beach

in the distance peas eaten the night before

still welding it together

the clay swan with a broken neck

best friend told me to think about it

forgot that I had one

from anus to morsel the

cut-off point as

your mother's ha ha

fucked up anecdote

laid the terms at his feet but

Jeff still couldn't get over it

What do you mean it didn't work

flat brush does as

flat brush wants

twink archipelago of

rainbow speckles

legs apart weight forward:

a snorkel and a snorkel vest

cucked and living in Britain

we put him away every year and

he blows up no problem

two Inflatable flowers one short

white one tall purple

you look into the flower and it

dissolves into brown bumpy disks

girl kisses monkey like she's done it before

the counterpoint the heart of the kernel

stuck in my teeth dancing in drought

transition to wear miniskirts in private

good art now that's

a dog chasing its own tail

and you what are you like

star formations wrap their

legs round the moment take a bite

out of this juicy pomegranate and

shut up for one second

Art-breath

fogs gallery windows

as Jeff shows New York how his objects

get stuck in a cunnilingus vortex

Gertrude said

sucking is dangerous work

early birds watch me

stack plastic chairs to

avoid time's mild abuse

the smell of blue water slides not far off

the burn it leaves a

meet-cute with nylon

alright let's go see

split-rocker

carpeted in plants

supposed to be headed to

an entertainment complex

in Arizona but

the most evangelical of irrigation systems

holding over twenty-five tons of soil

makes it difficult to transport

ah

heartbreak heartbreak heart

So sexy: the dialogue

between having control

and riding a speedboat

into an Inflatable

help me with these 3D scenarios

I need to figure out

where the runaway bride will go

I'm thinking somewhere with a deep purple

so somewhere like Kansas

other than the bear float that smelled of

honey it was all the same there was so

much space on the sidewalks

you could just stand there and

watch Honor make out the wind

what a joy to get away from

'normal' living conditions

in this tubular metallic structure

someone blows a soap bubble

across Jeff's face

exasperating Satan and by the way gross

play dad tacit quotation marks

your head on the table

your hand in your mouth play dead

off-screen voice says

dummying the plotline

less a thing

than the trace of movement

hand in hand with Michelangelo's erection

you put your head through plywood and

you're an astronaut but

you can't put

your head in an astronaut and

find chipboard

Barbie version of Mount Rushmore

was miles away

when I went one of the presidents

had turned his back to the public

great

throw a flower in the hat

and easily miss

Breathe and it smells of violets

baby dressed in lavender a

balloon's surface almost garish colours

highly polished toy elephant made into

a monumental sculpture

the orifice of the geyser is so smooth

but I don't expect

anyone to look and say oh that's a geyser

cherry whipped cream leaks into

the ship and Jeff's no help

dangling his buoyant heart

from a bow smiling coquettishly

if writing put a hole

through painting I still wouldn't do it

Change name before

it's too late

he put down Life without buildings

and I thought

not this again

some dim freeze

in Jeff's mind as

he paroles

a succession of

pop culture trophies

so dead...like

dip-moulding sex toys

but it got out of hand

now a whole

village of them

with his boundary

no longer material

my lungs the shape

of a heart every time

I see you

Dreamt I was a

curly-haired readymade ouch

not kissing and kissing colours

all the matchy matchy

bourgeois busts position themselves

as being better than

the 1950s pin-up girl

a prehistoric sculpture Jeff bought

off the internet honey look it is

both a sailboat and a vagina

you and your interactions

lying constantly I told

him this was beyond cultural recognition

the gradations the drawings

the gyrating pool toy

that kind of stuff

it's methodical work in the sense that

I tuft each letter into the poem

yet I have no desire to coldly work this

into another medium

I am here in a way

I find difficult to be anywhere else

a leech to the present tense

a toe to the stub

blisters from my coat

a 'Chance' encounter

at my very own show

the one where I celebrate

a Pink panther porcelain

feeling up a blonde

bombshell and

coming back to

what's left of the

sky when night falls

I couldn't stop thinking about

the way she tilts her head

like she's addressing an audience

his body hugs her chin

resting on her shoulder

mountain rescuer knocking on

Jeff's door

Although I cannot move this mountain

I can don my costume and make you a

balloon animal

we're here for you mr koons

from the rainbow beginning

you think of

maybe a rock star having

a split personality

it would be great to

just cut it down the

middle put them

together and then

place the bar back

through the handle

the pony has a cooler palette

but the dinosaur's red

curves May to October

Jeff laughing so hard he takes

his snot for a walk

trying to unpin the family photos

that's a screwdriver by the way

The same mickey mouse face

handed down

from generation to generation

sometimes cutting past each other

in line to the softball game

his grandfather was his father's father

and he was a really nice person

friendship as a method to getting what

you want help me push the pig into the

next poem lollipop in your mouth I'll

lick the insides of your cheek keep you warm

bite you like an 80's chew toy

king pig smooth cheeks

the pink colour of seams and puckers

Still he wanted to be famous

I told him photoshopping his penis

wouldn't change anything apart from

imbuing his penis with

gossip and run-of-the-mill fetish

is that all you think there is

in this climate of violent piety I changed my

name my sister edits videos of

us as kids

teenagers unleash thousands

of crickets in conference rooms

and every time

I think about it

I pull a hair

out of my mouth

RON PADGETT

SCARY MOMMY

I miss Phyllida Barlow I'm
into poems that do not describe anything
except themselves
there's another
spoon in there
somewhere
and
in my misunderstanding of the
procession of events I
walked up to the bride with my
own set of rings thought
the train arrived when it let another
one pass him by
do you want to leave
around the same time
hugging these stables
I'm feeling so faint
is this a rocking

horse or a cock-a-doodle

I'M A STAR SAID THE LAMB I'M KEIR STARMER SAID KEIR STARMER

Perched on a waist-high

stool at the bar

the nipples I find myself

in conversation with are

that of a sinister businessman

wearing a sweater with a zip

to display his cleavage

he leans back expectantly in

anticipation of

the high catastrophe

that's about to occur

led by Ron Padgett

sustained by

foam index fingers

his hand is a ball

of string my hand is

a safety net

designed

to provide whiffs

of a botched community

think about it

says

a tiny full man at the end

of this sneaky midnight

we've failed to drink through

you've been telling me

things I didn't

want to know

and I put my head

on my knees

my captain says

put your head

on your knees

and I put my head

on my knees

BANKSY TAGS A HORSE

Throughout our time
together: the chugging
the floral fantasy of puppies
the crisis the wilding
people have and always
will

solving
this problem
calls for something like snow, anchored in persona
alert to the rose and to
actual life, ironized and completely unbelievable
jealous of that animal twitch

one
christian mistake
later and
a string of puppies we
both hold
our relationship
to objects

a sculptural
installation our happiness
a bowl of cereal and milk
nice

I like that the works could
be melted down to
spoons

it's a trick taken from
autofiction that means
absolutely
nothing

Ben Lerner can be
a sort of tufting
what leads
you to say a thing like that
well it's platitudinal

it's unbetrayable
it's the white dot
on the puppy's nose

A VERY GRUMPY HARRY POTTER

Sheep folds in the distance I've been

flattened and flattened again

free open syllables in

the young father's studied indifference

reward me!

another paranoid centre with which to

cowboy build my life

and also a kind of play on

the everyday and we are living

a very bad dream he is definitely out

but it works when

you don't realize you're

in it

eight universes side

by side be the proof against

captain awesome

with all his facial features reduced

to a single eye and

that backwards bill cap is a sinkhole

leading to real life or rural

upstate New York

light-pink barbed wire at the

crest of one hill while you

fill a plastic bag with carrots